ABOVE THE RIM

HOW ELGIN BAYLOR CHANGED BASKETBALL

BY JEN BRYANT

ILLUSTRATIONS BY FRANK MORRISON

Abrams Books for Young Readers ● New York

ACKNOWLEDGMENTS

Sincere thanks to the following people, without whose guidance, support, and expertise this book would not have been born: Matt Zeysing, curator, and Alex Pedro, curatorial assistant, Naismith Memorial Basketball Hall of Fame, Springfield, Massachusetts; Carol Welch and Laura Salvucci, reference department, Chester County Library, Exton, Pennsylvania; the reference specialists at the Main Reading Room, Humanities and Social Sciences Division, Library of Congress, Washington, D.C.; Tamar Brazis and Howard Reeves, wise and patient editors at Abrams Books for Young Readers, New York; Rob Sternitzky, copyeditor; Pamela Notarantonio, art director; Frank Morrison, artist, who brought Elgin's story so brilliantly to life on these pages.

The illustrations in this book were created using oil on illustration board.

Cataloging-in-Publication Data has been applied for
and may be obtained from the Library of Congress.

ISBN 978-1-4197-4108-1

Text copyright © 2020 Jen Bryant
Illustrations copyright © 2020 Frank Morrison
Edited by Howard W. Reeves
Book design by Steph Stilwell and Max Temescu

Printed and bound in China
10 9 8 7 6 5 4 3 2 1

Abrams Books for Young Readers are available at special
discounts when purchased in quantity for premiums
and promotions as well as fundraising or educational use.
Special editions can also be created to specification. For details,
contact specialsales@abramsbooks.com or the address below.

Abrams® is a registered trademark of Harry N. Abrams, Inc.

ABRAMS The Art of Books
195 Broadway, New York, NY 10007
abramsbooks.com

To my agent, Alyssa E. Henkin, and her family
—J.B.

To the children who love basketball as much as I love painting
—F.M.

On a steamy summer day in 1945,
a boy and his brothers
played stickball in the street.

There were plenty of nice parks in Washington, D.C.,
where people swam or played tennis, basketball, and baseball.
But the child was black, and those parks were
"whites only."

Sometimes, late at night,
when the city was asleep,
the older boys tunneled under
the padlocked fences
and played there anyway.

But things can change in time,
the child knew.
Time was important.
That's why his own name, Elgin,
came from his father's favorite watch.

And this time, there was no "whites only" sign.
It wasn't fancy—just a place to play basketball.
A fine game of skill and strategy,
and of running back and forth—
a flat-footed game as level as the court itself.

Now Elgin and his friends could play it, too.
At first, they didn't have the right equipment,
so they played with a tennis ball.
Then someone found a volleyball.
Then, finally . . . Yes! A real basketball.

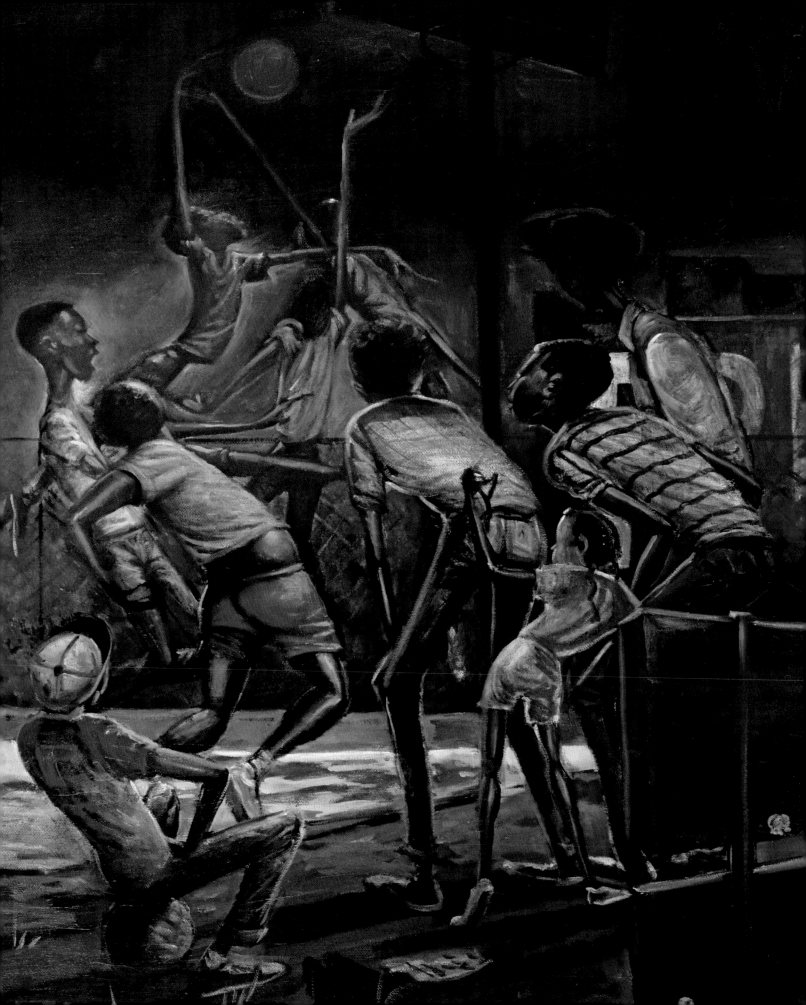

Some of the older boys were very good—and they knew it.
"Hey, you see that shot I made?" one bragged.
"That's nothin'—you see that shot I *blocked*?" another boasted.
"Oh yeah? Well, you just try to slide by me!" another challenged.

Elgin heard what they said.
But bragging was not his style.
On the court, he let his body
do the talking.

In one smooth move,
like a plane taking off,
he would leap . . .
higher and *higher*
and **higher**—
as if pulled by some
invisible wire,
and just when it seemed
he'd have to come down,
no!

He'd HANG there, suspended, floating like a bird or a cloud,
changing direction, shifting the ball to the other side,
twisting in midair, slashing, crashing,
gliding past the defense, up—up—above the rim.

And with a flick of his wrist,
or a roll off the fingertips,
he put the ball IN.

The *way* he played was so
different that people
stopped what they were doing
and watched.

"Where did he learn those moves?"
the other players asked.
Elgin didn't have an answer. "I don't know,"
he told them. "It's spontaneous."

Elgin grew taller and stronger.
He jumped higher and leaped *longer*!
His friends called him Rabbit.

At all-black Springarn High,
Elgin brought his outdoor moves inside.
He could score from anywhere on the floor—
a hanging jumper from the corner
or a drive inside spin-shot off the backboard.

"He's unstoppable!" the other teams complained.

"Go, Rabbit, go!" the fans cried
as Elgin leaped, turned, and twisted toward the rim,
or took on a defender one-on-one,
gave a quick head fake,
and reverse dunked *over* him!

Whenever Elgin played, people stopped what they were doing
and watched.

After high school, Elgin wanted to go to college,
But the D.C. colleges wanted "whites only."

"You should come out west," said a friend who went
to the College of Idaho.

So Elgin did.

It rained hard those first few days.
But when the skies cleared, it was time for a game . . .

And soon, people in Idaho
stopped what they were doing
and watched.

"No one else plays that way!"
the coaches declared.
"Where did he learn those moves?"
they wondered.
Elgin didn't have an answer. "I don't know,"
he told them. "It's spontaneous."

That winter, Elgin led his college team to victory.
And that winter, far away in Alabama,
a black woman named Rosa Parks sat down on a city bus
and refused to give up her seat to a white man.
That was a victory, too.

When people learned about Rosa on the news,
they stopped what they were doing and watched.

Later, Elgin
transferred to Seattle,
where he led his team
to the 1958 college
championship finals.
The newspapers wrote
a lot about Elgin.
They also wrote about
the courage
of the first black students
in Arkansas
to sit down in an all-white
classroom.

All across the country, people stopped what they were doing and watched.

In 1958, the Minneapolis Lakers chose Elgin Baylor first,
out of all the college players in the nation.
Elgin "Rabbit" Baylor was now a professional athlete.
But in those days, being in the NBA
was not like it is today.

Fans flocked to watch Major League Baseball . . .
But with only eight teams, the NBA had a hard time selling tickets.
The players didn't make much money.
They traveled long distances in loud, clickety-clack trains
and slept leaning over in their seats, their long legs jammed underneath.
Sometimes they flew in made-over cargo planes.

They played back-to-back nights and washed their uniforms
in hotel bathrooms.
They slept on beds that were too short.
They played when they were injured or sick.

Even so, Elgin played as hard as he could—
and so did his Lakers teammates.

Meanwhile, another team gathered
in the basement of a church in Wichita, Kansas.
They practiced sitting down and not fighting back,
even if they were bullied and harassed.

Later, they sat down at a "whites only" lunch counter
until they were served food.

CATER TO WHITES ONLY..

COLORED

But change came slower elsewhere.
That winter in West Virginia,
when the Lakers needed a place
to stay overnight, every hotel said
"whites only."
So Elgin and his teammates said,
"No thanks."

The whole team checked into Edna's guest
house, where anyone was welcome.
They were hungry. Where could they eat?
Downtown, all the nice restaurants were
"whites only."
Elgin bought some cold food at the
bus station and ate in his room.

That night, as the other players suited up and walked onto the court,
Elgin sat down before the crowd
without a uniform.
"Why isn't Elgin Baylor out there?" the reporters asked.
"It's not fair!" the fans complained. "We paid to watch the whole team!"

But his coach and his teammates understood.
They were with him at the hotel. They knew
he'd been turned away at restaurants.

"I'm a human being," Elgin told them.
"And I want to be treated like one."

Sometimes you have to sit down to stand up.
And that's what Elgin did.

The fans noticed. The newspapers noticed.
And . . . the NBA commissioner noticed.
A few weeks later, he made a new rule:
No NBA teams would stay in a hotel or eat in a restaurant
that practiced discrimination.

Elgin had already changed the way
basketball was played. Now, by sitting
down and NOT playing, he helped
change things off the court, too.

In 1959, Elgin was voted NBA Rookie of the Year.

Two years later, the Lakers moved to Los Angeles, California,
where famous people seemed to be everywhere!
Fame changed people, Elgin knew.
But it didn't change Elgin.

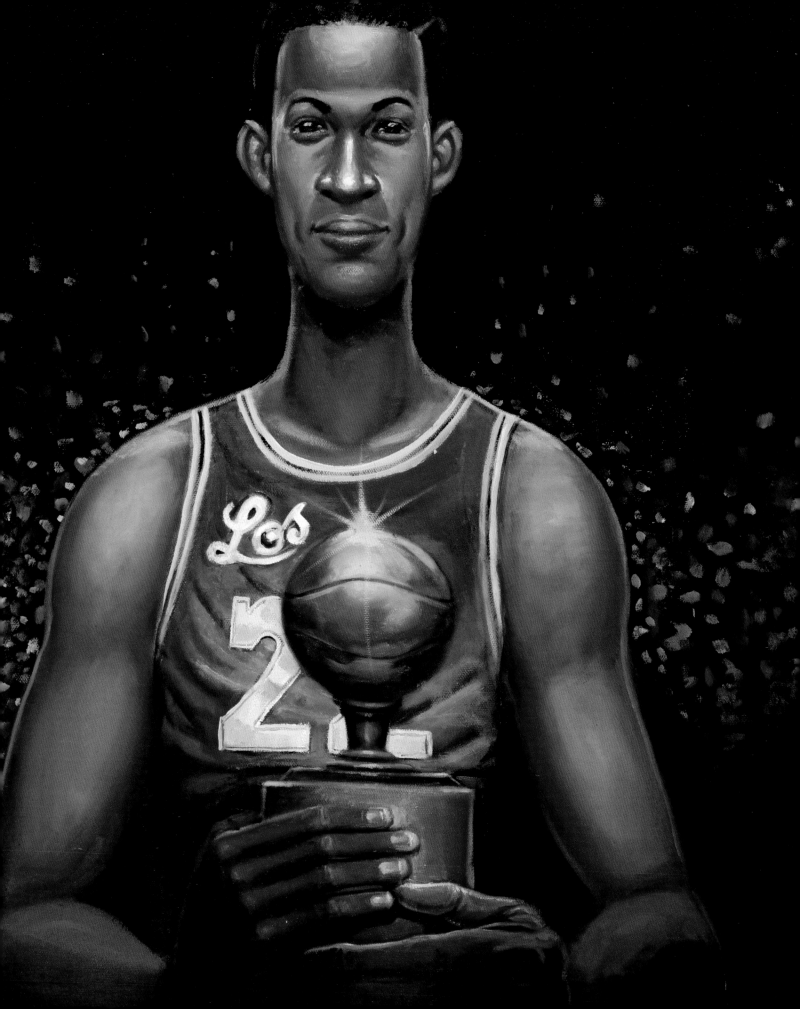

In one smooth move, like a plane taking off,
he leaped . . .
higher and *higher* and **higher**—
as if pulled by some invisible wire,
and just when it seemed he'd have to come down,
no!
He'd HANG there, suspended, floating like a bird or a cloud,
changing direction, shifting the ball to the other side,
twisting in midair, slashing, crashing,
gliding past the defense, up—up—above the rim.

And with a flick of his wrist,
or a roll off the fingertips,
he put the ball IN.

Wherever Elgin played, people stopped what they were doing and watched.

AUTHOR'S NOTE

As a lifelong participant in both sport and art, I believe that the basic principles of mastery and excellence are the same whether you're running a 10k race, composing a poem, pitching a fastball, or painting a mural. Many of my previous books have been about art and artists—and in many ways, this one is, too. Artists change how we see things, how we perceive human limits, and how we define ourselves and our culture. The great ones add whole new dimensions, expanding the definitions of their activities and providing models to be emulated by future generations.

NBA Hall of Fame player Elgin Baylor is such an artist, because he changed the way the game of basketball is played. Baylor did for basketball what Picasso did for visual art, what Martha Graham did for dance, and what William Carlos Williams did for poetry. He broke with tradition and ventured into uncharted athletic territory, altering the game profoundly and forever. He came to basketball late and, lacking any formal coaching or instruction before high school, created his own unique moves and shooting style.

This creativity, coupled with exceptional athletic ability and a fierce dedication to team play, made him a standout star in high school, in college, and in the NBA. In his 2013 autobiography, NBA Hall of Famer Julius "Dr. J" Irving recalled the first time he saw Baylor play on television, and the tremendous effect it had on him: "[Baylor gave] me an idea of how basketball could look effortless and beautiful. . . . there is scoring, putting the ball in the basket, but also the artistry of how it is done . . . I see [his] movement, reenact in my mind and I can't explain to anyone . . . why it excites me, but I see it as somehow liberating. . . . This is a new idea, [one] I have never heard spoken aloud."

Baylor's influence on the game is prodigious, and yet his contribution to basketball is often overlooked. Reasons for this include the racial bias surrounding professional sports and sports media coverage in the 1950s and 1960s; the fact that pro basketball wasn't nearly as popular as baseball or football in the years during which Baylor played; and Baylor's own humility and aversion to self-promotion, bragging, or any inflated sense of self-importance. These factors have allowed his unparalleled performance, statistics, and his unique stylistic contributions to basketball to remain largely unheralded.

Baylor's life on the court is only part of his story, however. His early experiences in segregated schools and athletic clubs, his journey west to colleges in Idaho and Seattle, his entrance into the NBA, his friendships with NBA teammates and rivals, his quiet but effective protest against racial discrimination—these were the building blocks of a humble man with extraordinary talent, an athlete who, with his unique artistry, inspired players such as Michael Jordan, Julius Irving, and LeBron James. It's my hope that this book will introduce the next generation to a great American athlete and shine a light on his legacy.

FURTHER READING

Baylor, Elgin, with Alan Eisenstock. *Hang Time: My Life in Basketball*. New York: Houghton Mifflin Harcourt, 2018.

Bayne, Bijan C. *Elgin Baylor: The Man Who Changed Basketball*. Lanham, MD: Rowman & Littlefield, 2015.

Daley, Arthur. "A Man Who Prized High Standards." *New York Times*, November 10, 1971.

Dwyre, Bill. "Jerry West and Elgin Baylor Are Together Again." *Los Angeles Times*, February 5, 2009; articles.latimes.com/2009/feb/05/sports/sp-dwyre5.

Gross, Milton. "Elgin Baylor and Basketball's Big Explosion." *Sport*, April 1961.

Hardman, A. L. "Segregation Ruling Ires Pro Player." *Charleston Gazette*, January 17, 1959.

Hudson, Dick. "Warming Up." *Charleston Daily Mail*. January 17, 1959.

McKenna, Dave. "Wilt vs. Elgin: When Their World Was the Playground. Two legends in the summer of '57." *Grantland*, August 28, 2012; grantland.com/features/the-legendary-pickup-basketball-games-wilt-chamberlain-elgin-baylor-late-1950s-washington-dc.

Olderman, Murray. "Elgin Baylor: One Man Franchise." *Sport*, April, 1959.

Pluto, Terry. *Tall Tales: The Glory Years of the NBA, in the Words of the Men Who Played, Coached, and Built Pro Basketball*. New York: Simon & Schuster, 1992.

Walters, Ron. "The Great Plains Sit-In Movement, 1958–1960" (1996) *Great Plains Quarterly*. Paper 1093; digitalcommons.unl.edu/greatplainsquarterly.

WEBSITES AND AUDIO RECORDINGS

Audio Recording of September 9, 1997, Interview by Ron Barr
blogs.loc.gov/loc/2014/03/sports-gold

Brief Biography from Naismith Hall of Fame
www.hoophall.com/hall-of-famers/tag/elgin-baylor

Statistics as Player, Coach, and Executive
www.basketball-reference.com/players/b/
bayloel01.html

Summary of Baylor's NBA Career and Statistics
www.nba.com/history/players/baylor_bio.html

"Top Five" Baylor Highlights with the NBA Lakers
www.lakersnation.com/video-top-5-elgin-baylor-
lakers-moments/2013/09/24

Wilt Chamberlain Archive—Archival Video
www.youtube.com/watch?v=rjNS_oYE92E

ESPECIALLY FOR YOUNG READERS

"Baylor, Elgin." *The Lincoln Library of
Sports Champions*. Cleveland, OH: Lincoln
Library, 2013.

Sports Illustrated Basketball's Greatest. Editors of
Sports Illustrated, October 21, 2014.

*Sports Illustrated Kids Slam Dunk! Top 10 Lists
of Everything in Basketball*. Editors of *Sports
Illustrated*, 2013.

NOTES

11, 16   "I don't know . . . It's spontaneous": Elgin
Baylor paraphrased, from Terry Pluto, *Tall Tales*,
page 192.

14   "He's unstoppable!": www.hoophall.com/hall-
of-famers/elgin-baylor.

16   "No one else plays that way!": Dave McKenna,
"Wilt vs. Elgin," bit.ly/2lPYiVi.

28   "I'm a human being . . . And I want to be
treated like one": John Taylor, *The Rivalry*. New York:
Ballantine, 2006; page 135.

28   *Sometimes you have to sit down to stand up*:
Paraphrased from JFK's campaign speeches in which,
praising the courage of student nonviolent actions
at lunch counters, he reportedly said: "The occasion
comes when sometimes you have to sit down to stand
up for your rights," in Dorothy Gilliam, "Symbolism,"
Washington Post/Proquest Historical Newspapers;
November 21, 1983: D1.

38   "[Baylor gave] me an idea . . . aloud." Julius
Erving, with Karl Taro Greenfield. *Dr. J.: The
Autobiography*. New York: HarperCollins, 2013; page 35.

TIMELINE

September 16, 1934: Elgin Gay Baylor born in
Caroline County, Virginia, the fifth and youngest child
of John and Uzziel Baylor. Nine days later, the family
returns to their home in Washington, D.C., where Elgin
will spend his childhood.

August 1936: At the Summer Olympics in Berlin,
Germany, U.S. Track & Field athlete Jesse Owens
wins gold medals in the 100 meters, 200 meters, long
jump, and 4×100 meter relay. His dominance on this
world stage completely disproves Hitler's idea of white
supremacy and enrages the German dictator.

March 21, 1946: Kenny Washington, a halfback from
UCLA, joins the Los Angeles Rams, becoming the first
African American to sign with an NFL team.

April 15, 1947: Jackie Robinson debuts with the
Brooklyn Dodgers, becoming the first black athlete
to play in Major League Baseball.

1948: Elgin Baylor plays basketball for the first time
at a new public park near his home.

April 25, 1950: Charles Henry "Chuck" Cooper is
drafted by the Celtics as the fourteenth overall pick.
He becomes the first African American to play in
the NBA.

September 1950–June 1952: Baylor attends
Phelps Vocational High School and plays on their
basketball team. Averaging 18.5 points per game as a
freshman, he leads them to the city's African American
championship game as a sophomore.

1951: Racial segregation in Washington, D.C., restaurants
is declared unconstitutional by the U.S. Supreme Court.

1952: Baylor temporarily drops out of school to work
in a furniture store, but continues to play basketball in
recreational leagues.

1952–1953: Transfers to all-black Springarn High
School. Leads their basketball team in scoring,
averaging 35 points per game.

1953–1954: As a senior, Baylor scores 63 points
against Phelps, breaking the citywide record.

March 12, 1954: Leads his all-black Stonewall Athletic
Club team to a victory over Jim Wexler's all-white
"Scholastic All-stars."

May 17, 1954: U.S. Supreme Court hands down a
unanimous decision in the case of *Brown v. Board of
Education*, declaring "separate educational facilities are
inherently unequal."

1954–1955: Attends College of Idaho; leads college team to undefeated season in their conference.

December 5, 1955: Rosa Parks is arrested for refusing to give up her seat to a white man on the city bus. This begins the Montgomery Bus Boycott, which lasts 381 days and results in the desegregation of the city's bus system on December 21, 1956.

1956–1958: Attends Seattle University and leads their basketball team to the NCAA finals in 1958.

January–February 1957: Dr. Martin Luther King Jr. and others establish the Southern Christian Leadership Conference. Inspired by both biblical texts and by the tactics of Indian Independence leader Mahatma Gandhi, the SCLC uses nonviolent protests to further civil rights.

July 6, 1957: Althea Gibson is the first African American to win Wimbledon.

September 1957: Nine black students challenge segregation in public schools by enrolling at all-white Central High School in Little Rock, Arkansas.

March 30, 1958: First performance of the Alvin Ailey American Dance Theater company in New York City.

April 22, 1958: Chosen by the Minneapolis Lakers as the number one draft pick in the NBA. Their previous season's record, 19 wins, 53 loses, was the worst in the NBA.

July 12–August 7, 1958: The Wichita, Kansas, youth council of the NAACP stages a sit-in at the Dockum drugstore. This three-week event successfully desegregates the city's lunch counters.

August 19, 1958: Youths in Oklahoma City, Oklahoma, begin a series of lunch counter sit-ins to protest racial discrimination.

October 22, 1958: Plays first professional NBA game as a Minneapolis Laker.

January 16, 1959: After being turned away at a Charleston, West Virginia, hotel and restaurant because he was black, Baylor refuses to play in that night's game against the Cincinnati Royals. Known for his work ethic and dedication to team play, Baylor's boycott underscores the extent to which racial discrimination is rampant both inside and outside the NBA.

1958–59 NBA season: Named NBA Rookie of the Year. Leads Lakers to the NBA finals, where they lose to the Boston Celtics. Appears in NBA All-Star game and is voted co-MVP.

1959–60 NBA season: Averages 29.6 points and 16.4 rebounds per game in-season, 33.4 points in the postseason.

February 1, 1960: Four college students stage a sit-in at the "whites only" Woolworth's counter in Greensboro, North Carolina. Intense media coverage inspires a multistate sit-in movement to protest segregation in hotels, restaurants, libraries, and other public spaces.

1960–61 NBA season: Lakers move from Minneapolis, Minnesota, to Los Angeles, California. Baylor leads the team in scoring, averaging 34.8 points per game. Along with rookie guard Jerry West, he helps to win thousands of new West Coast fans.

November 15, 1960: Scores a record 71 points (there was no three-point line until 1979) against the Knicks in New York. Has 25 rebounds that same night.

1961–62 NBA season: Spends six months stationed at Fort Lewis, Washington, as a member of the Army Reserves. When he's able to get a weekend pass, he flies all night to wherever the team is playing and joins them on the court. Despite missing regular team practices and a lot of sleep, he averages 38.3 points per game, and the Lakers make it to the NBA Finals.

1962–63 NBA season: Becomes the first player in NBA history to finish the season among the top five players in four categories: scoring, rebounding, assists, and free throws.

1963–64 NBA season: Begins to experience knee problems, which will continue for the rest of his career. Despite diminished playing time in the coming years, his on-court contributions allow the Lakers to reach the NBA finals five more times in the next six seasons.

1971–72 NBA season: After fourteen years in the League, Elgin Baylor retires after re-injuring his knee. He was an All-Star for eleven of those seasons (1959–65, 1967–70). His lifetime NBA statistics: 23,149 points (all pre-three-point era); 11,463 rebounds; 3,650 assists.

November 17, 1974: Appointed interim head coach by the New Orleans Jazz.

December 16, 1976–April 12, 1979: Serves as head coach of the New Orleans Jazz.

May 2, 1977: Inducted into the Naismith Memorial Basketball Hall of Fame (elected to the same in 1976).

1980: Named to the NBA 35th Anniversary All-Time Team.

1996: Named to the NBA 50th Anniversary All-Time Team.

April 15, 1986–October 7, 2008: Executive for the Los Angeles Clippers.

April 6, 2018: Bronze statue of Elgin Baylor unveiled at Staples Center, Los Angeles.

April 10, 2018: Publishes *Hang Time: My Life in Basketball*, with Alan Eisenstock.